YOU CHOOSE™
SURVIVAL

Can You Survive

ANTARCTICA?

An Interactive Survival Adventure

by Rachael Hanel

Consultant:
John Splettstoesser
International Association of Antarctica Tour Operators
Waconia, Minnesota

CAPSTONE PRESS
a capstone imprint

You Choose Books are published by Capstone Press,
1710 Roe Crest Drive, North Mankato, Minnesota 56003.
www.capstonepub.com

Library of Congress Cataloging-in-Publication Data
Hanel, Rachael.
  Can you survive Antarctica? : an interactive survival adventure / by Rachael Hanel.
    p. cm. — (You choose survival)
  Includes bibliographical references and index.
  Summary: "Describes the fight for survival while exploring Antarctica"—Provided
by publisher.
  ISBN 978-1-4296-6589-6 (library binding) — ISBN 978-1-4296-7345-7 (paperback.)
  1. Antarctica—Discovery and exploration—Juvenile literature. 2. Wilderness
survival—Antarctica—Juvenile literature. 3. Survival skills—Antarctica—Juvenile
literature. I. Title.
  G863.H36 2012
  919.8'9—dc22   2011007893

Editorial Credits
Angie Kaelberer, editor; Veronica Correia and Bobbie Nuytten, designers;
    Wanda Winch, media researcher; Eric Manske, production specialist

Photo Credits
Alamy: Arcticphoto/Bryan and Cherry Alexander, 53, 58, Classic Image, 12, Mary
Evans Picture Library, 18, Photos 12, 30; Corbis: Bettmann, 14, Science Faction/Jeff
Harbers, 89, Sygma/John Van Hasselt, 65, Sygma/Stéphane Cardinale, 47, 71; Getty
Images Inc: Central Press, 27, Gallo Images/Fiona McIntosh, 44, General Photographic
Agency, 42; John Splettstoesser, 91, 98; Seth White, 85; Shutterstock: Karen Kean, 6,
kkaplin, 8, pashabo, design element; SuperStock Inc: age fotostock, cover; United States
Antarctic Program/National Science Foundation: Emily Stone, 105, Kristan Hutchison,
74, Peter Rejcek, 77, 100, 103, Robert Schwarz, 61, Stacy Kim, 72

Printed in the United States of America in Stevens Point, Wisconsin.
022012   006602R

TABLE OF CONTENTS

About Your
ADVENTURE

YOU are traveling through the bleakest, coldest place on Earth—Antarctica. This place is like nothing you have ever experienced.

In this book you'll deal with extreme survival situations. You'll explore how the knowledge you have and the choices you make can mean the difference between life and death.

Chapter One sets the scene. Then you choose which path to read. Follow the directions at the bottom of each page. The choices you make will change your outcome. After you finish one path, go back and read the others for new perspectives and more adventures.

YOU CHOOSE the path you
take through your adventure.

Antarctica is considered
a desert, even though it
is covered with ice.

CHAPTER 1

The Last Place on Earth

Few places on Earth are as unforgiving, dangerous, and cold as Antarctica. Average summer temperatures on this continent that surrounds the South Pole are just 20 degrees Fahrenheit. The average winter temperature is -30 F and can plunge as low as -100 F. Raging blizzards seem to come out of nowhere.

Yet people have regularly traveled to Antarctica since the early 1900s. In the early days, adventurous men scrambled onto its icy surface to explore the unknown land. Later scientists went to the continent to learn more about weather, geology, and global warming.

Turn the page.

Adventurous travelers journey to Antarctica on cruise ships.

Today scientists and other workers live at the many research stations scattered about the continent. Even casual travelers board cruise ships that stop at Antarctica's shores.

Almost all travel to Antarctica takes place during its summer months, which are November to February. The cold and near-constant dark of the Antarctic winter make it difficult for humans to survive.

But dangers lurk all around even in summer. Snowstorms or just an overcast sky can make it impossible to see in front of you. What seems to be a clear path may hold hidden dangers, such as deep crevasses in the ice. The intensity of the sun's rays reflected off the snow can burn the corneas of the eyes, causing snow blindness.

Those traveling even for short periods outside may become victims of frostbite and hypothermia. Frostbite often occurs in fingers, feet, ears, and the nose. If it is not treated quickly, it destroys skin and tissue. Hypothermia, which occurs when the body's temperature gets too low, is often deadly.

Antarctica's isolation and remoteness can breed danger. No hospitals exist. Many research stations do have medical doctors. But if you aren't near a research station, it can take a long time to get help. Even something as simple as a toothache can become a serious problem.

Turn the page.

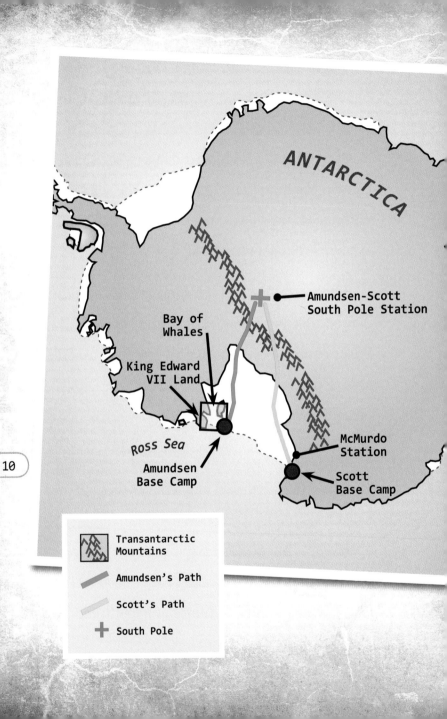

ANTARCTICA

Amundsen-Scott
South Pole Station

Bay of
Whales

King Edward
VII Land

Ross *Sea*

Amundsen
Base Camp

McMurdo
Station

Scott
Base Camp

Transantarctic
Mountains

Amundsen's Path

Scott's Path

South Pole

CHAPTER 2

Race to the Pole

The year is 1911. Many parts of the world still remain mostly untouched by humans. Adventurous people seek out these unexplored areas. They want to be the first to set foot on a new land.

Two teams of explorers are each quietly making plans to be the first to the South Pole. You have a chance to be on one of the teams. The South Pole is a bitterly cold and empty place. No people have ever lived there. The adventure could easily turn deadly. But reaching the South Pole first will bring fame and honor.

You must first decide what expedition you want to join. Roald Amundsen of Norway leads one team. Robert Falcon Scott of Great Britain leads the other.

Turn the page.

Scott loaded much of his team's gear on motorized sleds.

Amundsen's team is using skis and 115 sled dogs to travel. Scott is traveling using 19 Siberian ponies and 33 sled dogs. Scott's team also has a new invention—motorized snow sleds.

Scott is more familiar with the Antarctic terrain. He had first tried to reach the South Pole in 1902. But Amundsen is a more experienced polar explorer. He has spent much time in far northern Canada with Inuit villagers. He learned their ways of survival.

Which team do you think has the better chance to reach the South Pole first and survive the return journey?

To be a part of Amundsen's team, turn to page **16**.

To go with Scott, turn to page **18**.

You and the other members of Amundsen's team started this trip in October 1910. Beginning in February 1911, you place three supply depots along the beginning part of your route. Each depot contains about 2,000 pounds of food and fuel. The depots look like snow towers with the supplies tucked inside. A flag is placed on the top.

The depots are all in place by the end of March. You wait at Framheim, the base camp near the Bay of Whales, through the cold, dark, Antarctic winter. In September 1911 Amundsen is ready to start the journey. But you think September is too soon to start. Still, you leave with Amundsen and six others

on September 8, 1911.

The weather quickly turns ugly. Temperatures fall, and the wind picks up. The dogs' frostbitten feet make running painful. Just four days after starting, Amundsen decides to head back to Framheim and wait for better weather.

By September 15 you are just 40 miles from Framheim. But the numbing cold causes you and two other men to get frostbite in your feet. The tingling sensation sends ripples of pain through your body.

Amundsen takes off with two other men. He leaves the rest of you behind because the frostbite has slowed you down. You and the others are left out in the bitter cold with no food or fuel. You use the whip to keep your exhausted dogs going.

Soon after midnight on September 16, you and another teammate struggle into camp. Everyone else made it back hours before. You are angry. Amundsen's decision could have cost you your lives. You want to say something to Amundsen so he doesn't make the same mistake again.

To speak out, turn to page 22.

To keep quiet, turn to page 24.

You and the other Scott team members spend early 1911 laying down supplies such as food and fuel along the beginning of your route. You build depots out of the snow as high as you can, with the supplies inside of them.

But your team runs into problems. The motor sleds fail to perform in the cold weather. The Siberian ponies sink to their knees in the soft snow. Seven ponies die from exhaustion or accidents. You can't make it to the last depot location.

Supply depots (center) were placed along the expedition routes.

You leave the base camp at Cape Evans on November 1, 1911. Scott hopes for warmer weather by starting later in the Antarctic spring. He believes the ponies can travel farther in warmer temperatures.

The journey starts poorly. It snows heavily. Then warmer temperatures arrive, and the snow thaws. The soft, wet snow is difficult to trudge through. The remaining ponies are struggling to move. In early December they must be shot because they are slowing down the entire team.

There isn't enough food for everyone to make the journey to the pole. After the ponies are shot, Scott sends the dogs back to the base camp with some of the men. You will be pulling your sled and its 200-pound load yourself.

Turn the page.

On December 10 you reach the Beardmore Glacier. You pause for a moment to look at the task ahead of you.

The trek up the glacier takes all the energy you have. You struggle to lift one foot in front of the other in the deep snow. The winds swirl so much snow you can barely see. When the sun comes out, the glare off the snow causes you to become snow blind. You must rest every few minutes just to catch your breath. Some days you only travel half a mile.

On December 20 Scott sends four men back to base camp. You're relieved not to be among them.

You still have a chance to reach the Pole.

After more than two weeks, you finally reach the top of the glacier. Now it's a flat journey to the Pole. You hope it will be easier.

With just 180 miles to go, Scott decides to send back four more men. The sleds are lighter now, and there isn't enough food for eight men. Heading back now might save your life. But you also are eager for the glory that would come with being the first to the South Pole.

To keep going, turn to page **26.**

To turn back, turn to page **32.**

At breakfast the next morning, you confront Amundsen. "You are the team's leader," you tell him. "It is unthinkable that you left men behind. We nearly died. When we start again, you will have to make sure you take care of all of your men."

Silence fills the room. When Amundsen finally speaks, he is angry.

"I will not tolerate my men telling me what to do," he says. "I know what is best for us." He takes you aside. "I do not want you going with me to the Pole."

Your stomach drops. Amundsen says he is sending you in a smaller party to explore King Edward VII Land, a peninsula about 800 miles from the Pole. You'll bring two other men with you.

Your group sets forth around the same time Amundsen and four others go toward the South Pole. On the peninsula, you collect rocks and take photos. But toward the end of your journey, a fierce snowstorm strands you for several days. As a result, your supplies of food and fuel are running low. But you still have more exploring to do.

"I think we should head back," you tell your companions. "We have barely enough supplies to last a week. If we leave now, we can return to base camp before the supplies run out."

Turn to page 35.

At breakfast the next morning, you keep quiet. Someone else at your table speaks up. As he listens, Amundsen's face reddens with anger.

"I don't need critics like you on the trip to the Pole," he tells the man. "I will find another job for you."

Amundsen sends him to explore King Edward VII Land. This peninsula is about 800 miles from the South Pole. It is an interesting journey, but not as historic as your journey to the Pole.

You and three other men are going with Amundsen to the Pole. Amundsen calls a meeting.

"I need both dogsled drivers and skiers," he says.

A dogsled driver stands on a sled behind a dog team that is pulling the supplies. It is his job to make sure the dogs go where they are supposed to go.

A skier gets to travel lightly. He will go ahead and decide on the right path for the dogsleds.

"Both jobs require much responsibility. I want you to decide which you think will better suit you and the team," Amundsen says.

You are a good skier, and you are also good with dogs. What should you do?

To be a skier, turn to page 28.

To be a dogsled driver, turn to page 30.

Scott planned to take just three men with him. But at the last minute, he decides to bring you along for extra pulling power.

But Scott didn't plan for five people on this last leg of the journey. You're short one pair of skis, and Scott's tent only sleeps four. You're worried that you will run out of supplies. Five men use more food and fuel than four men.

You forget about those problems as you get closer to the Pole. You're almost there! As you get closer, you see something in the distance. It's a scrap of cloth tied to a pole.

"Could it be?" you ask Scott quietly. "Could the Norwegians have beaten us?"

You arrive at the Pole and see the Norwegian flag. Your suspicions are correct.

"We are not the first," Scott says sadly. "But we have made it. You all have done a good job."

You spend two days there. With a heavy heart, you start the return journey. The winds howl. The snow and ice cut into your face. One day you are not dressed properly for the sudden storm that appears. Your clothes are soaked.

Scott's team found Amundsen's tent and the Norwegian flag.

To put your clothes on the tent floor, turn to page 36.

To hang your clothes up in the tent, turn to page 38.

You enjoy the swoosh of your skis over the snow. The trip to the Pole is going well. You travel 15 to 17 miles per day.

But this job leaves you tired and hungry. You eat once at midday and again when you set up camp at night. You get a few more extra rations than the dogsled drivers, but it's still not much.

One night during your evening meal, you are in charge of food preparation. You look around to make sure no one is watching. You eat an extra biscuit and a portion of dried meat called pemmican.

But Amundsen sees you. He lectures you sternly. "We must be very careful to eat exactly what has been allowed. If you eat too much now, we won't have enough left for the return journey," he says.

You do have one option to eat more. Amundsen plans to kill 24 of the 42 sled dogs and save the meat for food. But if you kill some dogs, that will leave fewer dogs to pull the sleds and supplies. That could force you all into a dangerous situation.

To advise against shooting the dogs, turn to page 40.

To agree with Amundsen's decision, turn to page 42.

Sled dogs were a big part of Amundsen's plan to reach the Pole.

You enjoy the quiet of sitting behind the dogs as they run through the snow. The trip to the Pole is going well.

In the beginning you traveled just five or six hours each day so as not to tire the men or the dogs. You rested the dogs once each hour. You were able to travel 15 to 17 miles per day. You even crossed the Transantarctic Mountains. The dogs were a big help.

But now Amundsen has a plan for the remaining journey to the Pole and the return journey. He thinks you should kill 24 of the 42 dogs to provide food for the other dogs and for the hungry men who are on skis.

This is difficult news for you. You have grown close to the dogs. You feed them every day, take care of them, and give them commands to go forward. But Amundsen is your leader.

To refuse to help kill the dogs, turn to page 40.

To help shoot the dogs, turn to page 42.

To your surprise, Scott sends back only three men. You are one of them.

Five men are going to the Pole. Scott thinks the fifth man will provide more pulling power. But that leaves your team short one man. You will all have to pull heavier sleds with three people than you would with four.

You and your two companions begin your return journey on January 4. You climb over the same terrain and trudge through the same deep snow that you did the first time. You cover only a few miles each day.

The wind blisters your cheeks and fingers. Your feet and hands are so numb you can barely feel them. Your food supply is running low. Your stomach burns with hunger. Many times, you almost faint. But if you stop, you know you'll die. On February 19 you finally stumble into camp.

You rest for several days. You eat as much as you can. You wait for Scott and the four others to return. But as the Antarctic heads toward its winter, you realize that Scott's team isn't coming back. Even if they are still alive out there somewhere, they won't be able to survive the brutal winter.

You must wait several more months for the weather to turn warmer. While you wait, your heart sinks when you hear that Amundsen's team reached the Pole on December 14, 1911. They returned to their base camp in January.

In late October 1912, you set out with a search party to find Scott's team. On November 12 you discover Scott's tent buried in the snow about 11 miles south of the largest supply depot. Inside the tent are the bodies of Scott, Edward Wilson, and Henry Bowers, along with Scott's diary.

Turn the page.

You read the diary and learn that Edgar Evans and Lawrence Oates died before the other three reached their final camp. The diary's last entry is dated March 29. You are grateful that you survived the expedition, but mourn the loss of your leader and friends.

THE END

To follow another path, turn to page 11.
To read the conclusion, turn to page 101.

You look at the sky. Milky, fat clouds straddle the horizon. No doubt the snow will start to fall soon.

A strong blizzard forms as you leave. You struggle against the high winds and heavy snow. But your team is strong. In three days you travel 50 miles. By the end of the third day, the blizzard ends. You easily cover more than 20 miles a day in the good weather.

At the end of the week, you arrive at the base camp. Warm food and your comfortable beds await you. You were not part of the historic journey to the Pole, but you explored other parts of the harsh continent and survived.

THE END

To follow another path, turn to page 11.
To read the conclusion, turn to page 101.

You're tired when you get to the tent. You pile your clothes next to your sleeping bag. In the morning, they are still wet. You have no choice but to put them on.

"We must travel at least 15 miles a day to get back to camp before the weather worsens," Scott says.

Soon you realize that Scott didn't plan for bad weather. He planned only for the exact amount of food he thought your team would need, and you have an extra man. Also, you were not able to lay that last depot of food and fuel.

The men are sick, weak, and exhausted. Your head throbs. Blood trickles from your nose. All of you have nosebleeds from the high elevation.

Soon you fall behind the others. By the time they come back on skis to look for you, you are so confused that you don't even recognize them. The cold and starvation have taken their toll on your body. You feel the other men lift you up and carry you to the tent, but you can't speak.

"Let's give him some warm broth," one of your companions says. He lifts your head, and you try to drink. But you're too tired. All you want to do is sleep. That's the last thing you remember. You are the first of the five men to die on the return journey. Not one of you will make it back to camp.

THE END

To follow another path, turn to page 11.
To read the conclusion, turn to page 101.

You hang up your clothes in the tent. You think getting them off the floor will help them dry quicker. The next morning, the clothes are almost dry.

Scott wants to travel 15 miles a day in order to return to camp before winter begins. You find the depots that had been laid earlier. But there isn't enough food there. You feel weak and move slowly. You fall often. Your legs are bruised and sore from the falls. Temperatures plummet to -40 F.

Because you stayed dry, you fare a little better than the others. Edgar Evans is the first to die. He had severe frostbite and an infected accidental knife wound. Then one day Lawrence Oates leaves the tent. He says, "I'm just going outside, and I may be some time." You all try to stop him, but you are too weak. Now it's just the three of you.

By mid-March it's clear that you will not be able to make it to the next depot. You wished you had made different decisions. But nothing can be done about that now.

You all write letters to your families and leave them in the tent. Scott writes, "Had we lived, I should have had a tale to tell of the hardiness, endurance and courage of my companions which would have stirred the heart of every Englishman." It was a noble effort, but not one of you succeeded.

THE END

To follow another path, turn to page 11.
To read the conclusion, turn to page 101.

"I don't think that's a good idea," you tell Amundsen. "We will need all their power to get us to the Pole and back."

"But the dogs and the skiers are hungry," Amundsen says. "We will travel lighter and save on food if we do this. It must be done."

But you can't stand to shoot the dogs. You let your companions do it. You also refuse to eat the dog meat, even though you know it would give you much-needed energy.

There is little time to rest. You must push on to the Pole. In less than a month, your team arrives.

There is no sign that Scott was there. You are the first! Your names will go down in history. You cheer as Amundsen plants the Norwegian flag at the Pole.

You spend a couple of days at the camp before starting the journey back to Framheim. The well-placed depots along the way supply the food and fuel you need. You all arrive back at base camp alive.

But your decision not to eat the dog meat has left you weak. Your body will never be the same again. You live out your life in a weakened condition, but you still are a hero.

THE END

To follow another path, turn to page 11.
To read the conclusion, turn to page 101.

You help shoot the dogs. Some of the men refuse to take part. But you see no choice. You eat the meat and almost immediately feel better.

About three weeks later, on December 14, you finally reach your goal: the South Pole! And even better, there are no signs of Scott's team.

Crew member Helmer Hanssen celebrated with the sled dogs at the Pole.

"We are the first!" you yell. All five of you hug one another. Even the normally calm Amundsen smiles widely.

"Who wants to plant the Norwegian flag?" Amundsen asks.

You look at the others. They are silent. "You should plant it," you say. "You are our leader."

Amundsen places the flag at the Pole. He pitches a small tent. Inside he leaves letters that he wrote for the king of Norway and also for Scott.

After a couple of days of making observations, you head back to Framheim. The team has no problems finding the supply depots. You have enough fuel and supplies to successfully return. After several weeks, you and your team return to Norway as heroes.

THE END

To follow another path, turn to page 11.
To read the conclusion, turn to page 101.

Skiers exploring Antarctica pull their supplies on sleds.

CHAPTER 3

Women making History

You are about to make history. You are leading a group of four women skiing to the South Pole. No other group of women has done this before.

You plan a traverse of the continent. You will start at one end of Antarctica, travel to the South Pole, and then continue to the opposite coast. You'll travel a distance of 1,500 miles. You're all in this together. If for some reason one woman can't finish, the rest of you won't go on.

Turn the page.

The four of you have raised all the money for the trip. You are on a tight budget. The only way not to go over budget is to stick to a timeline. Your trip is planned to last three and a half months. A delay could make it more expensive to get home. It also puts you at risk of traveling during the dangerous Antarctic winter.

You choose your supplies carefully. You load up about 1,000 pounds of food for the trip, including cheese, beans, pasta, dried meat, and oatmeal. Chocolate, nuts, and dried fruit will be high-energy treats.

Your tents, sleeping bags, and clothes are made of materials such as polypropylene, polyester, and polar fleece. These materials are both lightweight and warm.

Survival equipment includes tents, stoves, and fuel.

You begin your journey on November 9. Immediately, a blizzard flares up. Do you press on and hope the storm ends soon? Or do you stay until it blows over?

To wait, turn to page 48.

To leave, turn to page 49.

Waiting proves to be a good decision. The storm lasts for a couple of days. As you huddle in your tent, you worry about the delay.

"Will we be able to make up this lost time?" asks your tentmate, Jill.

"Yes, I think so," you reply. "But we're going to have to go farther each day than we had planned. It will be tough." You had planned to cover about 5 miles each day in the beginning. You are pulling a 200-pound sled, so it's difficult to travel farther than that.

To push the pace, turn to page 54.

To make up time later, turn to page 56.

You wait only long enough for the storm to ease up a bit. By the time you pack up and load the sleds, snow is still whipping through the air. Your muscles ache from the weight of the 200-pound sled. As the trip continues, the sled will become lighter because you'll use up food, fuel, and other supplies. Then you'll be able to travel between 15 and 20 miles each day. But now the weight makes it hard to meet your goal of 5 to 6 miles per day.

After a couple of days, you develop a deep, hacking cough. You think it's bronchitis. The bitter cold, driving snow, and hard work have weakened your body. At night your cough wakes up Jill, your tentmate.

"Maybe we should have waited for the storm to pass," Jill says. "We've pushed too hard. I think we should rest here for a couple of days."

Turn the page.

"I would feel better after resting," you admit. "Then I could start strong and maybe go even farther each day."

But resting would put the whole group behind. What if the group doesn't reach its goal because of you?

To rest for a couple of days, go to page 51.

To keep moving, turn to page 52.

The other team members, Beth and Kristine, agree that you should rest.

"We could all use a break," Beth says. "We'll come back stronger."

After a full day and night of sleep, you feel much better. Your cough has almost disappeared. You must decide whether to make up the lost time now, or wait until later in the journey when your sleds will be lighter. Right now, you can travel 5 to 6 miles per day with the heavy sleds. But you could push yourself to go faster. If you increase your mileage now, you will get back on schedule sooner.

To increase the pace, turn to page **54.**

To stick with your original plan, turn to page **56.**

"I think I'll be OK," you say to Jill the next morning. "Let's keep moving. I'll take some medicine from the first-aid kit."

The first-aid kit contains several kinds of medicine. It also holds bandages and splints. Since you think you might have bronchitis, you take antibiotics.

Two days later, you feel much better. The cough is less noticeable and you have more energy. Your teammates give you a little extra oatmeal and cheese to make you stronger. After a hard day of pulling, the three other women set up the tents and the stove used for food preparation and heat so you can rest.

Two weeks later, you notice the food supplies are getting low. The antibiotics are also almost gone. What if someone else gets sick? There wouldn't be enough medicine for them.

You could use your radio to call for a helicopter to fly over and drop supplies. But that will cost more money—money you don't have.

To cross the continent before winter, skiers need to average 16 miles per day.

To arrange for a supply drop, turn to page **60**.

To decide against a supply drop, turn to page **64**.

It is not easy to pick up your pace, but you are strong and well rested. Each day you follow the same routine.

You wake around 6 a.m. and make breakfast on the camp stove. You put on your clothes, pack the gear, and are out of the tent by 8 a.m. It takes another 30 to 40 minutes to pack the sleds. You ski for about two hours, then take a 15-minute break. You ski single file. You do this until about 7 p.m, when you stop to set up camp and cook supper. You're in bed by 10 p.m.

Things are going well until one day, you look ahead and see Beth fall to the ground. You quickly ski to her.

"Ouch!" Beth says, grabbing her ankle. "I hope it's not broken."

As you touch the ankle, Beth winces in pain. Jill and Kristine ski to her side.

"We'll have to make camp here," you say. "There's no way she can keep going."

To rest before continuing, turn to page **58.**

To call off the journey, turn to page **63.**

You decide to continue with your original schedule. As your sleds become lighter, your speed should increase.

But when you are three weeks away from the Pole, you look at the supplies. Something seems wrong. "The food is running very low," you say. "We don't have enough to last us to the Pole."

"How did that happen?" Beth asks. "We've been eating exactly what we rationed."

"I must have miscalculated how much we need," you reply, shaking your head. How did this happen? You planned this expedition in every detail.

"What are our options?" Kristine asks.

You sigh and think over her question for several minutes. What can you do?

"We can eat less than we're eating now and try to make our food last until we get to the Pole," you reply. "We can pick up supplies there. Or we can try to arrange a food drop in a few days. I have the radio. I can call the base camp to arrange for a helicopter to fly over and drop food down to us. That will be expensive, though."

To arrange for a supply drop, turn to page **60**.

To decide against a supply drop, turn to page **64**.

Scientists have worked at the Amundsen-Scott South Pole Station since 1956.

After a few days of rest, Beth's ankle is less swollen. "We'll divide up your supplies and put them on our sleds," you tell Beth. "That way you'll have a lighter load to pull." That does the trick. You make great progress each day for several weeks.

On January 12 you see some tiny specks on the horizon. Your global positioning system (GPS) shows that you are getting close. What you see is the Amundsen-Scott research station at the South Pole. One more day of skiing, and you arrive! The scientists and workers at the South Pole station greet you with cheers and chocolate.

But you are only halfway through your journey. You still must travel across the other half of the continent. You all are exhausted, and Beth's ankle is still sore. In slightly more than a month, the last ship will leave the coast. If you don't make it in time, you will have to pay hundreds of thousands of dollars to arrange a plane trip home.

You gather the women together. "Let's sleep on it tonight. We'll make a decision about whether to continue in the morning."

To abandon your trip, turn to page **69**.

To continue, turn to page **70**.

You each need about 5,000 calories a day to give you the energy to ski all day. You turn on the radio and call the base camp each hour to report the latest weather conditions. Aircraft can't land if it's snowing or windy.

During a good stretch of weather, the helicopter lands safely. The pilots bring food and supplies. When you load the sleds the next day, you notice the extra weight. It makes it hard to travel more than 6 to 8 miles each day. You make slow but steady progress.

You arrive at the South Pole on January 13. The dozens of scientists and researchers stationed there are all outside to welcome you. They greet you with hugs. Some hand you chocolate and other treats.

After the fanfare, you go to a quiet place and gather with your team.

As many as 150 people work at the Amundsen-Scott station during the summer months.

"OK, this is just the halfway point," you say. "Do you think we should keep going, even though we're behind schedule?"

"The last ship out of the harbor leaves in just over a month, right?" asks Kristine.

You nod. "If we don't get there in time, we're going to have to pay about $500,000 to arrange for a plane to pick us up."

Turn the page.

Jill shakes her head. "That's money we don't have."

"The weather is going to get worse too," Beth says.

"That's true," you say. "But remember that this is our one shot to make history. No female team has ever crossed the entire continent. It will be an incredible challenge, but if you're prepared to go for it, we have a chance. Let's sleep on it tonight. We'll make a decision tomorrow morning."

To continue, turn to page 67.

To abandon the trip, turn to page 69.

You stop and rest for several days, but Beth's ankle isn't healing. You suspect the ankle might be broken. Your heart is heavy as you call another team meeting.

"I'm so sorry," Beth says. "I just don't think I can go on."

"You're right," you say. "If it gets worse, there is no one who can treat it. You need a doctor."

You use the radio to call the base camp for help. A helicopter swoops in to pick up you and your teammates. You may not have reached your goal, but you're proud that you tried. You vow to someday return to Antarctica and complete the trip you started.

THE END

To follow another path, turn to page 11.
To read the conclusion, turn to page 101.

"A supply drop is going to cost us too much money," you say. "We're only about three weeks from the Pole. This will be a tough journey on less food, but we can do it."

But after a few days, you all start to feel the effects of not eating enough. You have been eating about 5,000 calories a day, but now you're trying to live on half of that. You have little energy. Going even 5 miles a day proves difficult. You all have frequent headaches.

With two weeks left to get to the Pole, you call a team meeting.

"This isn't working as well as we had hoped," you say.

"But we've come this far," says Beth. "It's hard to give up now."

The harsh weather is just one enemy of Antarctic explorers.

"That's true," says Jill, with tears in her eyes. "But I think we all know that to keep going while we're weak could result in serious injury or illness."

"Let's face it," Kristine adds. "Death is a very real threat right now."

Turn the page.

You nod. "You're right. As the leader, I'm responsible for everyone. To stop now is a difficult decision. But in order to stay safe and save our lives, it's the right thing to do."

You call a helicopter for rescue. You are ending your Antarctic journey earlier than you had hoped. But traveling as far as you did is a great accomplishment—something most people in the world will never do.

THE END

To follow another path, turn to page 11.
To read the conclusion, turn to page 101.

You're going for the traverse—the trip across the entire continent. You'll be using UpSkis. These sail-like contraptions attach to your body. While you ski, the sail catches the wind. You hope the UpSkis will help you travel much farther each day.

The Upskis work OK, but you're skiing against the wind, so you don't travel as far as you had planned.

"It's clear we're not going to make the deadline," you tell the others. "We're going to miss the ship going out of the harbor. We'll have to call for the plane when we finish our journey."

You celebrate when you reach the coast. But the $500,000 you spend for the airplane to pick you up casts a cloud on your good mood.

You arrive home as heroes. You travel the country speaking to organizations and schools. But you also have a huge debt that will take many years to pay off. Still, you're glad that you followed your dream.

THE END

To follow another path, turn to page 11.
To read the conclusion, turn to page 101.

The next morning, you gather your team together. Their faces are somber.

"I'm afraid we will not be able to do the traverse," you say. "The risk of something going wrong is too great. I will call for a helicopter to pick us up."

Beth, Jill, and Kristine nod in agreement, although there are tears in their eyes. If you keep going, everyone's lives would be at risk. Your decision to not continue is difficult, but wise.

THE END

To follow another path, turn to page 11.
To read the conclusion, turn to page 101.

The four of you meet in a quiet place to talk over your options. You ask the other women for their opinion s.

"Let's go for it!" Jill says. "I think we're all feeling pretty strong."

Beth and Kristine nod in agreement. "We at least have to try," Beth says.

"And we have the UpSkis," you add. An UpSki is a sail you attach to your body as you ski. The wind catches the sail, carrying you farther faster.

You all set out. To your relief, the Upskis work perfectly. You feel like you're sailing over a vast white ocean. The closer you get to the coast, the happier everyone feels. The difficulties of the earlier journey are almost forgotten.

UpSkis use the wind to increase a skier's speed.

You reach the coast in time to catch the ship. It's time for another celebration. You have become not only the first female group to reach the South Pole, but also the first female group to travel across the entire continent. You are brave, courageous role models for generations of women.

THE END

To follow another path, turn to page 11.
To read the conclusion, turn to page 101.

Researchers use devices with underwater cameras to study marine life.

CHAPTER 4

A Modern-Day Adventure

You are a research assistant who studies cold weather. You're starting an exciting mission. You will live and work at the Amundsen-Scott South Pole Station. Modern technology has made it possible for people to travel and stay in Antarctica. During the Antarctic summer, as many as 150 people live and work at the research station.

But one thing hasn't changed since the days of the early explorers. Antarctica remains a vast wilderness. Travelers still face great danger. Blizzards strike without warning. Giant crevasses lurk underneath thin layers of snow. Making the right decisions is the key to survival.

73

Turn the page.

Emperor penguins are found only in Antarctica.

You arrive at the South Pole and meet your new boss, Jim Potter.

"Welcome to the base!" he says, clapping you on the back. "I hope you're ready."

"I'm excited to be here," you reply.

"That's great," Potter says. "I could use your help in a couple of different ways. You could stay here at the station and help investigators in their drilling and collection of ice cores. The ice samples can contain information on the history of Earth's climate. This information helps scientists learn about today's global warming."

He pauses. "Also, some of our scientists need an assistant for emperor penguin research on one of the continent's islands. You will have to travel away from the base for a few weeks. But some people like getting away from the base, although a trip can pose a little more danger than staying here."

*To study the penguins, turn to page **76**.*

*To stay at the base, turn to page **78**.*

It would be fun to see more of Antarctica. Plus, the nearly 4-foot-tall emperor penguins are one of the few animals that can be studied in a habitat untouched by humans. Scientists study what effect climate change has upon the penguins. In turn, that can help them understand how climate change might affect people.

You board a small airplane with zoologist Wayne Campbell and six other researchers. The plane takes you 900 miles from Amundsen-Scott station to the McMurdo Station, an American research base on the coast of the Ross Sea.

From there, two trips are planned to the nearby island. You can take another plane ride, which will get you there more quickly. Or you can go to the island by boat, which is slower but possibly safer. The weather and extreme cold of Antarctica can affect a plane's performance while taking off, flying, and landing.

Small airplanes help researchers travel through the Antarctic.

U.S. ANTARCTIC PROGRAM

To travel by plane, turn to page 79.

To travel by boat, turn to page 81.

There's enough exciting work at the South Pole station to keep you busy. After a month, you eagerly await the plane that will bring food and other needed supplies. You look forward to a few treats, such as fresh fruit from New Zealand. But the day the plane is due to land, Jim Potter rushes into the lab. His face is pale.

"What's wrong, Jim?" you ask.

"The supply plane had to make a crash landing!" he exclaims. "One of the pilots left a radio message. They are not too far away. We need to send some people to rescue them. We also need a team here to coordinate the rescue effort and listen to the radio messages. What do you want to do?"

To join the search, turn to page 82.

To stay behind and coordinate the rescue effort, turn to page 83.

78

You board the LC-130 aircraft, which is equipped with skis for landing on ice. There are no seats. You sit on a bench along the plane's wall. The ride is bumpy and rough. After about an hour, an unexpected snowstorm begins. Strong winds rock the plane back and forth.

"Brace yourself for a water landing!" the pilot shouts over the intercom. You put on the life jacket that is under your seat and put your head between your knees.

Boom! The plane lands roughly in the water but holds together. It bobs in the water a few yards from shore. You're all able to leave the plane quickly. But the shock of the icy water sends shivers throughout your body. The temperature is around 10 F.

79

"Get to shore!" Campbell shouts. You swim furiously toward land. It's only a short distance, but moving your arms and legs in the icy ocean is almost impossible.

Turn the page.

You arrive on the shore, exhausted and breathless. You're at great risk for hypothermia. You know you should remove your wet clothes and huddle with the others for warmth as you wait for rescue. The pilot had just enough time to radio for help before the crash. But some of the other passengers are already weak and almost unresponsive. They need help.

To remove your clothes before helping the others, turn to page 88.

To help the others first, turn to page 90.

A few other researchers also decide to take the boat. It takes about a day to reach the island.

"We're glad you're here!" says zoologist Sarah Jones when you arrive. "Come with me to the rookery to observe the baby penguins."

You spend many hours at the rookery. You walk around and grow warm under your many layers, despite the cold temperatures. You take off your outermost coat and your gloves.

By the time you're finished observing the penguins, you can't even feel your fingers. They are waxy and white. You recognize the symptoms as frostbite. What is the best way to treat it?

*To warm your hands gradually, turn to page **92**.*

*To rub your hands to generate heat, turn to page **93**.*

You and four other workers join the search. You grab a rope and other rescue supplies. You pile on many layers of clothing—a light wool base layer to trap heat, a windproof jacket, and over all of that, a thick parka. You wear two pairs of thermal underwear as well as a pair of snow pants. The pilot is able to communicate by radio, so you know exactly where the crashed plane is located. You should get there in about an hour by snowmobile.

But suddenly the wind picks up and snow begins to fall. In just minutes, a blizzard is raging. It's impossible to see through the thick snow whipping around you.

"Quick!" you shout. "Everyone stop!"

To stay put until the storm lifts, turn to page **85**.

To continue the mission, turn to page **95**.

You monitor the radios and communicate with both the pilots and the rescue team. After about an hour, the rescue team finds the pilots, who are safe and unhurt.

Your time at the station is almost over as the Antarctic summer draws to a close. One day scientist Ann Smith tells you about an exciting opportunity. "As you know, a few of us stay here during the winter," she says. "It's a small group, but we do some important work. Are you interested?"

You are happy to have this opportunity, so you say yes. In the winter, the sun never comes over the horizon. But this allows you to see the beautiful aurora australis, the Southern Lights. The pink, green, and yellow lights dance in the sky like fire.

Turn the page.

Even in winter, the South Pole station is active with scientists, mechanics, and maintenance workers. At night you relax by watching movies, reading books, and listening to scientists give lectures on their findings.

But temperatures sink to -80 F and sometimes even lower. On a routine trip outside to check some equipment, you forget your gloves. In just a few minutes, your fingers are cold and white. You're in the beginning stages of frostbite.

To gradually warm your fingers, turn to page 92.

To put on gloves and rub your fingers together, turn to page 93.

You know from your winter survival training that you shouldn't try to keep going in a blizzard. "Let's dig a snow trench!" you shout to Joe, the man next to you. He passes the word to the other rescuers.

You all stop. Those of you who brought shovels dig into the snow as deep as you can. Others use snowshoes to dig. You carve out a narrow trench about 5 feet deep.

Snow trenches can help stranded people stay alive in the Antarctic.

Turn the page.

You lie down in the trench for protection. The wind blows over the trench, but you stay warm. It's a good thing you put on many layers of clothing.

The blizzard stops in a few hours. You're able to continue with the rescue. When you reach the crash site, the pilot and co-pilot are huddled in the wreckage. Amazingly, their injuries aren't serious, but they need to get out of the cold. The pilot rides on your snowmobile, while Joe takes the co-pilot. Soon you're back at the base.

In a few weeks, you get the opportunity to leave the base and go on a field mission. One field mission will collect meteorites. The other mission will go to the Transantarctic Mountains. This range separates the western and eastern parts of the continent.

To go to the mountains, go to page 87.

To study meteorites, turn to page 97.

You, four scientists, and several other assistants travel 350 miles to the base of the Transantarctic Mountains by snowmobile. There you set up your camp.

One day you travel with two scientists, Carlos Castillo and Anita Singh, to a nearby mountain. You ski there, pulling a small sled behind you. The snow is smooth. You're making good progress as you pull ahead of the two scientists.

"Slow down!" Singh calls to you. "This land is treacherous. You need to be more careful!"

You're a good skier, and you're enjoying the day. Why should you slow down?

To listen to Singh, turn to page **98**.

To keep your fast pace, turn to page **99**.

"Let me get out of my wet clothes first, and then I will help," you tell the others.

You take off everything but your thermal underwear. This will allow your skin to dry. You help team members who are having a hard time undoing zippers and buttons.

Once everyone is out of his or her wet clothes, you look around for shelter. You spot a rocky area near the shore. "Over here!" you shout. There you huddle together and wait for rescue.

About two hours later, the weather clears and the rescue plane arrives. Your body temperature is starting to drop. But removing your wet clothes and huddling together has kept all of you warm enough to prevent hypothermia.

In 1973 a C-130 Hercules airplane crashed near the South Pole.

The rescue plane brings you all back to McMurdo Station. Two days later you take another plane back to the Amundsen-Scott South Pole Station. You decide to stay at the station for the rest of your trip. One rescue is enough for you.

THE END

To follow another path, turn to page 11.
To read the conclusion, turn to page 101.

You decide to help the others. In a few minutes, you will have some time to attend to yourself.

But removing wet clothes from people who are almost unconscious takes longer than you expected. After just several minutes, your fingers are numb and becoming frostbitten. You manage to remove some layers, but not all of them. You huddle with the others for warmth in a rocky area on shore as you wait for rescue.

But you are not staying warm. In fact, you feel like you're getting colder. As the hours pass, you can't stop shivering. When you speak, your words don't come out correctly. And you're so tired. You just want to go to sleep.

"Hey, don't fall asleep!" Campbell says, grabbing your arm. "You need to stay awake!"

But you barely hear him. The rescue plane arrives and takes you to get medical attention.

But it's too late. You fall into a coma and die of hypothermia. The wet, cold clothes prevented your survival in the Antarctic.

Frostbite is just one danger of exposure to the extreme cold.

THE END

To follow another path, turn to page 11.
To read the conclusion, turn to page 101.

You know it's best not to rub your fingers together. The action might damage the tissue even more. Instead you put your hands in your armpits. You hope your body heat will warm your fingers.

You go inside the shelter and stand in front of a stove. You warm some shirts by the stove and then wrap them around your hands. It takes a couple of hours, but sensation slowly returns to your fingers. Your fingers burn, but you know that they're going to be OK. You treated the frostbite correctly and just in time. Your remaining time in Antarctica goes off without a hitch.

THE END

To follow another path, turn to page 11.
To read the conclusion, turn to page 101.

You put your gloves on. It seems to make sense to keep your fingers covered. You go into the shelter, stand next to the stove, and rub your hands together vigorously. After about a half an hour, your fingers don't feel any warmer. In fact, they feel and look even worse. One of the scientists, Sarah Jones, sees what you're doing and takes a look at your fingers.

"This is frostbite," Jones says. "We need to get these tight gloves off and wrap your hands in warm, loose clothing. The last thing you want to do is rub your fingers together. That can damage the tissue."

Jones warms the clothes by the stove and applies them to your hands. She does this for several hours, but you still can't feel your fingers. "A doctor will have to take a look at this," she says.

93

Turn the page.

The weather is good enough to allow a rescue plane to land within a few hours. The plane takes you back to McMurdo Station, where you see a doctor. But the frostbite is too advanced. The doctor must perform an emergency amputation of three of your fingers. For the rest of your life, you suffer the effects of your poor decision.

THE END

To follow another path, turn to page 11.
To read the conclusion, turn to page 101.

You continue with the rescue mission. You all creep forward slowly on your snowmobiles. But in the whiteout conditions, you lose your sense of direction. You start to panic as you realize that you can't see any of the other rescuers.

"Help!" you shout. "I'm lost! Where are you?" But the strong wind swallows your voice. Your group can't see or hear you. They don't know you have become separated from them.

You decide to stop and dig a snow trench, hoping it will protect you from the wind. You scoop out snow as deep as you can with your small shovel and lie down in the trench. But even with the walls of snow surrounding you, you become colder and colder. You start shivering and can't stop. You try to stay alert, but your brain seems frozen and sluggish as well.

Turn the page.

Suddenly, though, you start to feel warm. You begin pulling off layers of clothing and tossing them aside. You don't realize that the effects of hypothermia have reached your brain, making you think that you're not cold. Finally, you sink down into the snow again. As you close your eyes, you don't realize that you'll never open them again.

THE END

To follow another path, turn to page 11.
To read the conclusion, turn to page 101.

You take the field trip to study meteorites that are embedded in the snow and ice. Your camp stove provides heat. The tents are surprisingly warm and comfortable.

You spend a week gathering meteorites. The scientists are pleased with what you have found.

"This will help us discover more about our solar system," says scientist Carlos Castillo. "These might be the best samples we have ever found."

You return to the South Pole station and spend the rest of the season helping the scientists. Sooner than you would like, your Antarctic trip is drawing to a close. You enjoyed your time in the wilderness. You plan to return as soon as you can.

THE END

To follow another path, turn to page 11.
To read the conclusion, turn to page 101.

Singh is right. This area is full of dangerous crevasses, many hidden by snow. You slow your pace. Soon you notice an indentation in the snow. It's a crevasse!

"There's a crevasse here!" you shout. Carefully, you all go around the crevasse. You breathe a sigh of relief. You're glad that you slowed down and took the time to be aware of your surroundings. It likely saved your life.

Crevasses are a huge danger to Antarctic travelers.

THE END

To follow another path, turn to page 11.
To read the conclusion, turn to page 101.

You keep skiing at the same pace. Suddenly, your legs fly out from under you, and your body plunges down. You've hit a crevasse! You should have known that this landscape might be full of hidden crevasses.

The rope attached to your sled catches on the edge of the crevasse, preventing you from falling all the way down. The scientists hurry to you.

"Hang on!" says Castillo. "I'm going to get another rope."

Just then, your rope loosens. "I'm going to fall!" you scream. Singh tries to grab the rope, but it's too late. You fall 30 feet into the dark crevasse. Your carelessness has cost you your life.

THE END

To follow another path, turn to page 11.
To read the conclusion, turn to page 101.

On both land and sea, survival depends on good decisions.

CHAPTER 5

A Guide to Survival

Do you have what it takes to survive in Antarctica's harsh and unforgiving climate? Survival on the frozen continent depends upon many things. For one, you have to be physically fit. Your body can withstand the harsh Antarctic climate only if it's in top physical condition.

Mental toughness is just as important as physical strength. You must always think clearly. The best way to think clearly is to remain calm. Although some situations can be scary, it does no good to panic. In Antarctica, panicked thoughts can lead to deadly actions.

Careful planning will also help to make an Antarctic adventure successful. People who travel to Antarctica plan for months or even years before they leave. Many decisions can help increase your odds of survival. For example, you have to arrive during Antarctica's spring or summer, when the weather is at its best. You must bring the right clothing. You must become familiar with cold weather and the dangers it can bring.

Do you know enough about hypothermia? What are its symptoms? How do you treat it? Do you have the right footwear that will help prevent falls? If you plan on traveling outside, do you know how to recognize dangerous crevasses? Do you know the best way to help someone who has fallen into a crevasse?

Ladders and ropes are used to rescue people who fall into crevasses.

In Antarctica, small problems can quickly become life-threatening. An infection or a broken bone that is easy to treat at home requires special care in Antarctica. You should be prepared for any situation.

Many adventurers have traveled to Antarctica. Survival in this wild place poses an exciting challenge. Sadly, many people have gone to Antarctica and have not returned. But many others have traveled there and have returned to tell their stories of adventure. Those stories inspire others to do the same thing. Perhaps they will inspire you. With enough knowledge and preparation, you may have what it takes to survive Antarctica.

The Antarctic is a dangerous but beautiful place.

REAL SURVIVORS

Apsley Cherry-Garrard

Cherry-Garrard survived Robert Scott's ill-fated
expedition to Antarctica in 1911–1912. During the winter
of 1911, Cherry-Garrard was one of three men to take a
70-mile winter journey to Cape Crozier to collect emperor
penguin eggs. Temperatures sunk as low as -60 F. The
men also faced dangerous crevasses and raging blizzards.
They were near death when they returned from their
journey. Cherry-Garrard wrote a book of his experiences
titled *The Worst Journey in the World*.

Douglas Mawson

Mawson, a British explorer, survived a deep plunge into
a crevasse in 1913. He had started his journey with two
companions. Both died, and Mawson had to travel 100
miles by himself. He killed his sled dogs for food and
made the journey on foot. He fell 14 feet into a crevasse
before his rope caught on the edge. By sheer courage,
strength, and will, he slowly pulled himself up.

Ernest Shackleton

The story of British explorer Shackleton is perhaps the
greatest Antarctic survival story. In 1914 Shackleton was
on a quest to be the first to cross the Antarctic continent.
His ship, *Endurance,* was surrounded by ice shortly after
leaving the island of South Georgia. Shackleton and his
crew were stranded there for 480 days. Miraculously, not
one of the 28-man crew died.

Keizo Funatsu

Funatsu was a member of the International Trans-Antarctic Expedition of 1989–1990. With just 16 miles left of the 3,725-mile journey, Funatsu became separated from the others during a blizzard. He survived by digging a trench in the snow and doing exercises every 20 to 30 minutes to stay warm. After a long night, his teammates found him.

Jerri Nielsen FitzGerald

FitzGerald was the only doctor at the Amundsen-Scott South Pole Station in 1999. In May she discovered a lump in her breast. She performed a biopsy on the lump herself and found that it was cancerous. Through e-mail exchanges with other doctors and medical supplies that were flown in, she was able to start chemotherapy treatment. But it was clear she needed to get expert medical attention to save her life. In a daring rescue, a plane landed on October 16 and carried her away from the station. It was the earliest plane rescue in South Pole history. FitzGerald wrote a book about her experiences titled *Ice Bound*. She died of cancer in 2009.

SURVIVAL QUIZ

1. If you have frostbite on a body part, how should you treat it?

A. Vigorously rub the body part to restore the circulation.

B. Do nothing. It will recover on its own.

C. Warm the body part slowly and gradually.

2. What should you do if your clothes get wet and you can't get indoors quickly?

A. Remove your clothes and huddle with other people for warmth.

B. Keep your clothes on and drink hot tea.

C. Remove only your outer layer of clothing.

3. What is the best diet for a person traveling in Antarctica by ski or sled?

A. Lots of carbohydrates, such as fruit, bread, and sweets.

B. A mixture of high-protein and high-carbohydrate foods, such as dried meat, oatmeal, cheese, beans, and dried fruit, to provide energy and calories.

C. An all-meat diet.

Answers: C, A, B

READ MORE

Bledsoe, Lucy Jane. *How to Survive in Antarctica.* New York: Holiday House, 2006.

Friedman, Mel. *Antarctica.* New York: Children's Press, 2009.

Sohn, Emily. *Rescue in Antarctica: An Isabel Soto Geography Adventure.* Mankato, Minn.: Capstone Press, 2010.

Walker, Sally M. *Frozen Secrets: Antarctica Revealed.* Minneapolis: Carolrhoda Books, 2010.

INTERNET SITES

Use FactHound to find Internet sites related to this book. All of the sites on FactHound have been researched by our staff.

Here's all you do:
Visit *www.facthound.com*
Type in this code: **9781429665896**

GLOSSARY

antibiotic (an-tee-bye-OT-ik)—a drug that kills bacteria and is used to cure infections and disease

bronchitis (brahn-KYE-tiss)—an illness of the throat and lungs

crevasse (kruh-VASS)—a crack in an ice sheet or glacier that is hidden by a layer of snow

depot (DEE-poh)—structures holding supplies laid out in regular intervals

hypothermia (hye-puh-THUR-mee-uh)—a lowered body temperature that can be deadly

meteorite (MEE-tee-uhr-ite)—a rock originating in outer space that survives entry into Earth's atmosphere

pemmican (PEH-mih-kuhn)—a mixture of dried meat and fat that is a rich source of protein

peninsula (puh-NIN-suh-luh)—land that is surrounded by water on three sides

rookery (ROOK-er-ee)—a breeding area for penguins

traverse (TRAH-vurse)—a journey across an entire area

BIBLIOGRAPHY

Amundsen, Roald. *The South Pole (Vol. II).* London: John Murray, 1913.

Bixby, William. *The Race to the South Pole.* New York: Longmans, Green, 1961.

Huntford, Roland. *The Last Place on Earth.* New York: Modern Library, 1999.

Legler, Gretchen. *On the Ice: An Intimate Portrait of Life in McMurdo Station, Antarctica.* Minneapolis: Milkweed Editions, 2005.

Loewen, Nancy, and Ann Bancroft. *Four to the Pole! The American Women's Expedition to Antarctica, 1992–93.* North Haven, Conn.: Linnet Books, 2001.

Ponting, Herbert G. *The Great White South: Travelling with Robert F. Scott's Doomed South Pole Expedition.* New York: Cooper Square Press, 2001.

"Race to the End of the Earth." American Museum of Natural History. 11 April 2011. www.amnh.org/exhibitions/race/index.php.

Scott, Robert Falcon. *Scott's Last Expedition.* New York: Dodd, Mead, 1964.

"A Special Report: U.S. South Pole Station." National Science Foundation. 11 April 2011. www.nsf.gov/news/special_reports/livingsouthpole/intro.jsp

INDEX